WOULD YOU RATHER?

BIBLE EDITION

WELCOME

THANKS FOR PURCHASING THIS BOOK. WE LOVE TO CREATE BOOKS TO THAT HELP KIDS AND ADULTS LEARN MORE ABOUT THE BIBLE. THIS BOOK AIMS TO BRING THE FAMILY ALL TOGETHER TO DISCUSS TOPICS OF THE BIBLE IN A FUN WAY.

HOW TO PLAY

PLAY WITH A MINIMUM OF TWO PLAYERS. CHOOSE THE FIRST PLAYER THAT WILL ASK THE QUESTION THAT BEINGS WITH WOULD YOU RATHER? AND PROVIDE THE TWO SCENARIOS TO CHOOSE FROM. THE SECOND PLAYER HAS TO CHOOSE ONE AND EXPLAIN WHY.

CONTENTS PAGE

BATTLES OF THE
BIBLE

WOULD YOU RATHER BE SWALLOWED UP BY A FISH OR GO TO NINEVEH TO PREACH?

WOULD YOU RATHER FACE GOLIATH OR 10 MEN?

WOULD YOU RATHER FACE
PHARAOH OR THE RED SEA?

WOULD YOU RATHER WALK
SEVEN TIMES AROUND
THE WALLS OF JERICHO
OR ATTACK THE CITY
PHYSICALLY?

WOULD YOU RATHER
SUFFER AFFLICTIONS WITH
THE PEOPLE OF GOD OR
LIVE A LIFE OF LUXURY IN
PHARAOH'S PALACE?

WOULD YOU RATHER GO TO
BATTLE WITH THE OTHER
KINGS OR REMAIN IN
JERUSALEM AND WALK ON
THE ROOF OF THE KING'S
HOUSE?

WOULD YOU RATHER SUPPORT MOSES BY HOLDING UP HIS HANDS FOR HOURS TO WIN THE BATTLE OR GO PHYSICALLY TO FIGHT AT THE BATTLE GROUND?

WOULD YOU RATHER FIGHT THE MIDIANITES WITH 300 MEN, CLAY POTS AND TRUMPETS OR FIGHT AN ARMY WITH THE JAWBONE OF A DONKEY BY YOURSELF LIKE SAMSON?

WOULD YOU RATHER WITNESS THE BATTLE OF JERICHO OR THE BATTLE BETWEEN DAVID AND GOLIATH?

WOULD YOU RATHER BE KING DAVID'S THREE MIGHTY MEN WHO FOUGHT THROUGH THE RANKS OF THE PHILISTINES TO BRING HIM WATER FROM THE WELL AT BETHLEHEM OR DAVID'S MIGHTY MAN WHO SLEW A LION IN A PIT ON A SNOWY DAY?

THE LIFE OF
JESUS CHRIST

WOULD YOU RATHER DEFEND JESUS CHRIST OR ALLOW HIM TO GO TO THE CROSS?

WOULD YOU RATHER CLIMB THE SYCAMORE TREE AND WATCH JESUS CHRIST PASS OR INVITE HIM TO YOUR HOUSE?

WOULD YOU RATHER SIT AT
THE FEET OF JESUS LIKE
MARY OR PREPARE HIM A
MEAL LIKE MARTHA?

WOULD YOU RATHER TOUCH
THE HEM OF JESUS' GARMENT
AND BE HEALED, OR BE
THE FIRST IN THE POOL OF
BETHESDA TO BE HEALED?

WOULD YOU RATHER BE MARY MAGDALENE AND THE OTHER MARY AT THE TOMB WHERE THEY ENCOUNTERED AN ANGEL AFTER JESUS RESURRECTED, OR THE TWO DISCIPLES ON THE ROAD TO EMMAUS WHEN THEY ENCOUNTERED JESUS AFTER HIS RESURRECTION?

WOULD YOU RATHER GIVE YOUR LUNCH OF BREAD AND FISH FOR JESUS TO MULTIPLY OR EAT YOUR LUNCH YOURSELF?

WOULD YOU RATHER EXPERIENCE
THE HEALING POWER OF JESUS
WHEN PETER CUT OF THE EAR OF
A SOLDIER AND JESUS HEALED
IT OR THE DELIVERING POWER OF
JESUS WHEN AN UNCLEAN SPIRIT
WAS CAST OUT OF A BOY?

WOULD YOU RATHER SEE JESUS
TEACHING IN THE TEMPLE AS A
CHILD, OR BE PRESENT FOR HIS
FIRST MIRACLE OF TURNING THE
WATER INTO WINE?

WOULD YOU RATHER WITNESS
JESUS TURNING WATER TO WINE
OR FEEDING THOUSANDS WITH
BREAD AND FISH?

WOULD YOU RATHER HEAR JESUS
TEACH THE SERMON ON THE
MOUNT WITH THOUSANDS OF
OTHERS IN PERSON, OR LISTEN
TO HIM TEACH HIS PARABLES
TO A MORE INTIMATE GROUP OF
PEOPLE IN PERSON?

TRIALS AND TRIBULATIONS

WOULD YOU RATHER BE
SWALLOWED BY A FISH OR
DROWN IN THE SEA?

WOULD YOU RATHER HAVE
LEPROSY OR BE COVERED IN
SORES?

WOULD YOU RATHER BE COOPED UP IN AN ARK WITH TONS OF ANIMALS OR UNJUSTLY THROWN IN PRISON FOR TWO YEARS?

WOULD YOU RATHER BE DAVID FACING GOLIATH OR DANIEL FACING THE LIONS DEN?

WOULD YOU RATHER BE
DELIVERED FROM SIN BY WAY OF
THE GREAT FLOOD OR BY WAY OF
YOUR CITY BEING BURNED UP?

WOULD YOU RATHER BE IN THE
DESERT WITH NO WATER OR HAVE
SO MUCH QUAIL THAT IT COMES
OUT YOUR NOSTRILS?

WOULD YOU RATHER TRUST GOD TO RAISE YOUR ONLY SON BACK TO LIFE AFTER HE COMMANDED YOU TO SACRIFICE HIM OR TRUST GOD TO RAISE YOUR ONLY SON BACK TO LIFE AFTER HE FELL ILL AND DIED?

WOULD YOU RATHER ENDURE THE PLAQUE OF LICE OR THE PLAQUE OF FLIES?

WOULD YOU RATHER SPEND THE NIGHT IN THE LION'S DEN OR RECEIVE 39 LASHES?

WOULD YOU RATHER BE LOCKED IN STOCKS AND BONDS IN PRISON FOR YEARS OR BE SOLD INTO SLAVERY BY YOUR BROTHERS?

LIFE OF MOSES

WOULD YOU RATHER BE THE LEADER OF A MILLION PEOPLE OR FOLLOW A LEADER FOR 40 YEARS?

WOULD YOU RATHER PLEAD WITH GOD TO FORGIVE HIS CORRUPTED PEOPLE OR BE GOD'S SPOKESPERSON THAT TELLS PHARAOH TO LET HIS PEOPLE GO?

WOULD YOU RATHER LIVE
COMFORTABLY IN THE LUXURY
OF PHARAOH'S PALACE OR
STRUGGLE WITH THE ISRAELITES?

WOULD YOU RATHER BE COVERED
WITH FROGS OR FLIES?

WOULD YOU RATHER SEE THE MIRACLE OF MOSES LEADING THE CHILDREN OF ISRAEL ACROSS ON DRY GROUND THROUGH THE PARTED RED SEA, OR SEE THE ANIMALS ENTER THE ARK ON THEIR OWN AND WITHOUT A FIGHT?

WOULD YOU RATHER FACE DARKNESS FOR 3 DAYS OR HAVE BOILS ALL OVER YOUR BODY?

WOULD YOU RATHER BE CALLED
BY GOD TO ENTER A MOUNTAIN
THAT WAS COVERED IN THICK
BLACK CLOUDS WITH THE EARTH
THUNDERING AND SHAKING OR
SENT BY GOD TO CONFRONT
PHARAOH?

WOULD YOU RATHER BE AARON
AS THE SPOKESPERSON FOR
MOSES OR MOSES AS THE
SPOKESPERSON FOR GOD?

WOULD YOU RATHER WANDER IN THE DESERT FOR 40 YEARS WITH A REBELLIOUS PEOPLE, OR BE ON THE BACKSIDE OF THE DESERT TENDING SHEEP FOR 40 YEARS?

WOULD YOU RATHER THROW YOUR ROD DOWN AND WATCH IT BECOME A SNAKE, OR HOLD YOUR ROD OUT OVER THE RED SEA AND WATCH IT PART?

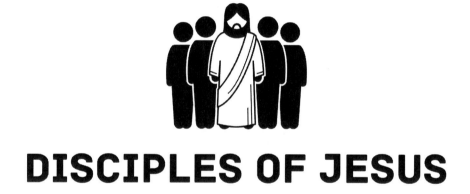

DISCIPLES OF JESUS

WOULD YOU RATHER BELIEVE THE REPORT OF THE RISEN CHRIST OR WAIT TO TOUCH HIS SCARS?

WOULD YOU RATHER EAT THE LAST SUPPER WITH JESUS OR HAVE BEEN PRESENT AT HIS BIRTH?

WOULD YOU RATHER ALLOW THE WOMAN TO ANOINT JESUS' FEET WITH EXPENSIVE OIL OR THE SELLING OF THE OIL TO HELP THE POOR?

WOULD YOU RATHER ASK JESUS TO ALLOW YOU TO WALK ON WATER LIKE PETER OR STAY WITH THE OTHER DISCIPLES IN THE BOAT?

WOULD YOU RATHER DOUBT THE RISEN CHRIST LIKE THOMAS OR BELIEVE LIKE THE OTHER DISCIPLES?

WOULD YOU RATHER BE CALLED BY JESUS FROM A LIFE OF A FISHERMAN, OR BE CALLED BY JESUS FROM A LIFE OF A TAX COLLECTOR?

WOULD YOU RATHER PULL A COIN FROM A FISH'S MOUTH OR PULL UP SO MANY FISH IN YOUR NETS THAT THEY BREAK?

WOULD YOU RATHER HEAR JESUS TEACH THE SERMON ON THE MOUNT, OR BE THE AUTHOR OF ONE OF THE BOOKS OF THE NEW TESTAMENT?

WOULD YOU RATHER CAST OUT A DEVIL WITH A WORD OR LAY HANDS ON A SICK PERSON AND SEE THEM BE INSTANTLY HEALED?

WOULD YOU RATHER WITNESS JESUS ASCEND INTO THE CLOUDS OR WALK THROUGH A WALL?

CHARACTERS

WOULD YOU RATHER HAVE THE PATIENCE OF JOB OR THE WISDOM OF SOLOMON?

WOULD YOU RATHER PERFORM THE MIRACLES OF ELIJAH OR ELISHA?

WOULD YOU RATHER BE KNOWN FOR YOUR INTEGRITY LIKE JOSEPH OR BE KNOWN FOR YOUR MEEKNESS LIKE MOSES?

WOULD YOU RATHER WRITE SONGS LIKE DAVID, OR PARTICIPATE IN THE WALLS FALLING DOWN WHILE BLOWING TRUMPETS AT THE WALLS OF JERICHO?

WOULD YOU RATHER HAVE
DINNER WITH PAUL OR SOLOMON?

WOULD YOU RATHER HAVE GONE
TO WAR WITH DAVID OR JOSHUA?

WOULD YOU RATHER HAVE LUNCH
WITH ESTHER OR RUTH?

WOULD YOU RATHER WRITE
SONGS LIKE DAVID OR WRITE
LETTER LIKE PAUL?

WOULD YOU RATHER CHOOSE YOUR OWN WAY LIKE ORPAH OR FOLLOW YOUR MOTHER IN LAW LIKE RUTH?

WOULD YOU RATHER LIVE IN THE WILDERNESS LIKE DEBORAH THE JUDGE OR MIRIAM THE PROPHETESS?

MIRACLES IN THE OLD TESTAMENT

WOULD YOU RATHER HAVE WITNESSED THE WATER FLOWING FROM THE ROCK OR THE SERPENT HEALING THE NATION OF ISRAEL?

WOULD YOU RATHER HAVE WITNESSED WIDOWS OIL MULTIPLIED OR THE SHUNAMMITE'S SON RAISED?

WOULD YOU RATHER HAVE
WITNESSED SHADRACH,
MESHACH AND ABEDNEGO
DELIVERED FROM THE FIERY
FURNACE OR DANIEL IN THE DEN
OF LIONS?

WOULD YOU RATHER SEE THE
WALLS OF JERICHO FALL OR
WATCH SAMSON CARRY AWAY
THE GATES OF THE CITY?

WOULD YOU RATHER HAVE THE STRENGTH OF SAMSON TO KILL A LION, OR THE MEEKNESS OF MOSES?

WOULD YOU RATHER WITNESS THE VALLEY OF DRY BONES BEING RESTORED INTO AN ARMY, OR WITNESS JOSHUA TELLING THE SUN AND MOON TO STAY STILL?

WOULD YOU RATHER WITNESS
RAVENS FEEDING ELIJAH,
OR MANNA FALLING FROM
THE HEAVENS TO FEED THE
ISRAELITES?

WOULD YOU RATHER BUILD THE
ARK THAT WITHSTOOD THE EARTH
BEING FLOODED OR WITNESS THE
WALL JERICHO FALLING?

WOULD YOU RATHER BE STUCK AT THE TOWER OF BABEL AFTER GOD CONFUSED THE LANGUAGES OR BE STUCK IN THE BELLY OF A BIG FISH FOR DISPLEASING GOD?

WOULD YOU RATHER BE THE KING WHO GOD ALLOWED TO LIVE AN EXTRA 15 YEARS OR SEE ALL THE GREAT PEOPLE OF THE CITY OF NINEVEH REPENT AND BE SPARED GOD'S JUDGEMENT?

MIRACLES IN THE NEW TESTAMENT

WOULD YOU RATHER HAVE WITNESSED HEALING OF THE CENTURION'S SERVANT OR HEALING OF THE WOMAN WITH THE ISSUE OF BLOOD?

WOULD YOU RATHER HAVE WITNESSED JESUS CHRIST FEEDING THE 5000 OR WALKING ON WATER?

WOULD YOU RATHER HAVE WITNESSED JESUS RAISING THE WIDOW'S SON OR HEALING OF THE 10 LEPERS?

WOULD YOU RATHER HAVE WITNESSED JESUS CALMING THE STORM OR HEALING OF JAIRUS' DAUGHTER?

WOULD YOU RATHER BE ONE
OF THE TEN LEPERS WHO WERE
HEALED OR ONE OF THE BLIND
MEN THAT WERE HEALED?

WOULD YOU RATHER BE LET
OUT OF PRISON BY AN ANGEL
OR FREED FROM PRISON BY AN
EARTHQUAKE?

WOULD YOU RATHER HAVE
WITNESS THE SERVANT OF A
ROMAN CATHOLIC HEALED OR A
PARALYTIC MAN HEALED ON THE
SABBATH?

WOULD YOU RATHER HAVE
WITNESS PHILLIP BEING
TRANSPORTED AFTER PREACHING
TO AN ETHIOPIAN EUNUCH OR
JESUS TURNING WATER TO WINE?

WOULD YOU RATHER HAVE
WITNESS DEMONS BEING CAST
OUT OF A PERSON OR PETER
MIRACULOUSLY FREED FROM
PRISON?

WOULD YOU RATHER FIND A COIN
IN A FISH MOUTH TO PAY FOR
TEMPLE TAX OR MIRACULOUSLY
CATCH 153 FISH IN YOUR NET?

LIFE OF PAUL

WOULD YOU RATHER HAVE SUNG
SONGS OF PRAISE IN PRISON
OR WRITE LETTERS TO VARIOUS
CHURCHES?

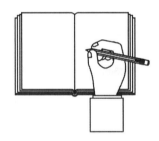

WOULD YOU RATHER HAVE
PREACHED THE GOSPEL TO THE
JEWS OR TO THE GENTILES?

WOULD YOU RATHER BE
A FAMOUS, ACCLAIMED
THEOLOGIAN, OR SUFFER
PERSECUTION FOR FOLLOWING
CHRIST?

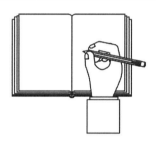

WOULD YOU RATHER SURVIVE THE
BITE OF A DEADLY SERPENT OR
SURVIVE THE DESTRUCTION OF
YOUR BOAT IN THE SEA DURING A
STORM?

WOULD YOU RATHER RECEIVE 39 STRIPES OF BE BEATEN WITH RODS?

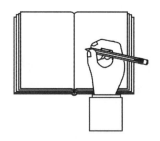

WOULD YOU RATHER THE SPIRITUAL FATHER TO TIMOTHY OR PREACH THE GOSPEL KING AGRIPPA?

WOULD YOU RATHER BE RESPONSIBLE FOR WRITING THE MAJORITY OF THE NEW TESTAMENT, OR BE RESPONSIBLE FOR ESTABLISHING THE MOST CHURCHES IN THE NEW TESTAMENT?

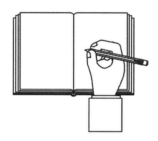

WOULD YOU RATHER HAVE THE WRITING ABILITIES OF PAUL OR FAITH OF PAUL?

WOULD YOU RATHER CONTINUE TO PERSECUTE THE CHURCH OR ACCEPT THE CALLING OF GOD?

WOULD YOU RATHER BE HEALED BY PETER'S SHADOW OR BE HEALED BY AN ANOINTED HANDKERCHIEF?

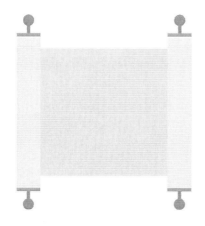

PROPHETS

WOULD YOU RATHER HAVE
WITNESSED THE MIRACLES OF
ELIJAH OR ELISHA?

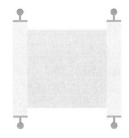

WOULD YOU RATHER HEAR THE
VOICE OF GOD AS A CHILD LIKE
SAMUEL OR BE KNOWN AS THE
PROPHET OF ISRAEL?

WOULD YOU RATHER PROPHESY THAT IT WILL NOT RAIN UNTIL YOU SAY SO OR PRAY FIRE DOWN OUT OF HEAVEN THAT CONSUMES THE SACRIFICE?

WOULD YOU RATHER WITNESS ELIJAH GO UP IN A CHARIOT OF FIRE, OR WITNESS ELISHA SMITE THE WATERS OF THE RIVER JORDAN WITH ELIJAH'S MANTEL AND WATCH THE WATERS PART?

WOULD YOU RATHER OVERSEE
THE REBUILDING OF THE WALLS
OF JERUSALEM OR OVERSEE THE
REBUILDING OF THE TEMPLE?

WOULD YOU RATHER WITNESS
THE HAND THAT WROTE ON
THE WALL AT BELSHAZZAR'S
BANQUET, OR KNOW WHAT JESUS
WROTE IN THE SAND WHEN THE
WOMAN CAUGHT IN ADULTERY
WAS BROUGHT TO HIM?

WOULD YOU RATHER BUILD A SPECIAL ROOM IN YOUR HOME FOR THE PROPHET OF GOD, OR OFFER THE PROPHET OF GOD THE LAST OF YOUR FOOD AND WATER?

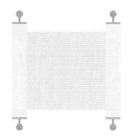

WOULD YOU RATHER DISOBEY THE KING'S COMMAND AND PRAY LIKE DANIEL, BEING THROWN INTO A LION'S DEN OR RUN TO PRESERVE YOUR LIFE FROM THE QUEEN'S COMMAND LIKE ELIJAH?

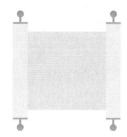

WOULD YOU RATHER USE COW DUNG TO COOK YOUR BREAD OR WALK THE STREETS NAKED LIKE EZEKIEL?

PROVEBRS

WOULD YOU RATHER BE HUMBLE OR EXALT YOURSELF IN LIFE?

WOULD YOU RATHER RESPOND TO THE WORDS OF A FOOL OR KEEP QUIET?

WOULD YOU RATHER HAVE
ADDITIONAL YEARS ADDED TO
YOUR LIFE, OR GREATER PEACE?

WOULD YOU RATHER FORGIVE
A THIEF WHO STOLE BECAUSE
HE WAS HUNGRY, OR SHOW
ACCEPTANCE FOR A PERSON WHO
GAINED TREASURES THROUGH
WICKEDNESS?

WOULD YOU RATHER BE BLESSED WITH WISDOM OR RICHES?

WOULD YOU RATHER OTHERS THINK OF YOU AS A POOR BUT KIND OR RICH BUT WICKED?

WOULD YOU RATHER HAVE
PATIENCE OR BE QUICK TO REACT?

WOULD YOU RATHER HAVE THE
RIGHT WORDS IN SEASON OR A
SOFT ANSWER THAT DEFUSES
CONTENTION?

WOULD YOU RATHER HAVE COMMON SENSE OR BEAUTY?

WOULD YOU RATHER HAVE A GREAT REPUTATION OR GREAT RICHES?

GENESIS

WOULD YOU RATHER HAVE WITNESSED THE CREATION OF DAY AND NIGHT OR THE SKY?

WOULD YOU RATHER HAVE WITNESSED THE STARS AND THE MOON BEING CREATED OR THE DRY LAND SEAS AND THE PLANTS?

WOULD YOU RATHER HAVE
WITNESSED THE CREATION OF
THE SEA CREATURES OR THE
ANIMALS THAT LIVE ON LAND?

WOULD YOU RATHER SACRIFICE
YOUR ONE AND ONLY SON AS GOD
COMMANDED OR BE TRICKED INTO
MARRYING THE WRONG SISTER?

WOULD YOU RATHER RECEIVE A COVENANT THAT GOD IS GOING TO GIVE YOU A LAND AND OFFSPRING AS THE SANDS OF THE SEA, OR WITNESS THE MIRACULOUS BIRTH OF YOUR ONLY CHILD AT 100 YEARS OLD?

WOULD YOU RATHER SELL YOUR BIRTHRIGHT IN A MOMENT OF WEAKNESS (ESAU), OR LOSE YOUR FAMILY FOR DECADES BECAUSE OF BEING DECEPTIVE (JACOB)?

WOULD YOU RATHER WRESTLE
WITH AN ANGEL AND GET
PERMANENTLY INJURED BUT
RECEIVE A BLESSING FROM
GOD, OR HAVE THE ABILITY TO
INTERPRET DREAMS?

WOULD YOU RATHER HAVE THE
PRESTIGE OF BEING SECOND IN
COMMAND IN ALL OF EGYPT, OR
HAVE THE JOY OF BEING ABLE TO
SAVE YOUR ENTIRE FAMILY FROM
FAMINE?

WOULD YOU RATHER LIE LIKE ABRAHAM WHEN HE TOLD PHARAOH THAT SARAH WAS HIS SISTER, OR LIE LIKE SARAH DID WHEN THE ANGELS SAID SHE WOULD CONCEIVE AND SHE LAUGHED, BUT THEN DENIED IT?

WOULD YOU RATHER BUILD AN ARK FOR MANY YEARS OR ENJOY THE PLEASURES OF LIFE?

RUTH

WOULD YOU RATHER HAVE LEFT YOUR MOTHER-IN-LAW IF YOU WERE RUTH OR STAY WITH HER?

WOULD YOU RATHER HAVE WORKED IN THE BARLEY FIELD IF YOU WERE RUTH OR STAY AT HOME?

WOULD YOU RATHER HAVE
SHARED THE BARLEY THAT YOU
HAD PICKED IN THE FIELDS WITH
YOUR MOTHER-IN-LAW OR NOT?

WOULD YOU RATHER HAVE
LISTENED TO THE ADVICE OF YOUR
MOTHER-IN-LAW NAOMI TO SEEK
MARRIAGE WITH BOAZ OR NOT?

WOULD YOU RATHER MOVE TO A FOREIGN LAND AND ADOPT YOUR MOTHER-IN-LAW'S WAY OF LIFE, OR STAY IN YOUR OWN LAND WHERE EVERYTHING IS ALREADY FAMILIAR TO YOU?

WOULD YOU RATHER RECEIVE SPECIAL TREATMENT OR WORK HARD FOR EVERY BIT OF FOOD YOU GATHER?

WOULD YOU RATHER CONTINUE
TO CALL NAOMI BY HER NAME OR
MARAH (BITTER)?

WOULD YOU RATHER MARRY
SOMEONE FROM YOUR OWN
COUNTRY OR THE RIGHT PERSON
GOD PROVIDES?

WOULD YOU RATHER PERSUADE
YOUR SISTER TO COME WITH YOU
AN YOUR MOTHER IN LAW OR LET
HER CHOOSE HER OWN PATH?

WOULD YOU RATHER MARRY
SOMEONE WITH WEALTH OR A
SIMPLE KIND, CARING PERSON?

ESTHER

WOULD YOU RATHER HAVE LISTENED TO THE ADVICE OF MORDECAI TO GO TO THE INNER COURT OF THE KING OR BE REJECTED?

WOULD YOU RATHER HAVE PREPARED A BANQUET FOR THE KING AND HAMAN OR NOT?

WOULD YOU RATHER HAVE
ACCEPTED HAMAN TO BE HANGED
OR FORGIVEN?

WOULD YOU RATHER BE VASHTI,
WHO HELD ON TO HER DIGNITY EVEN
THOUGH SHE WAS DISMISSED AS
THE QUEEN, OR BE ESTHER, WHO
WAS FACED WITH THE INCREDIBLE
RESPONSIBILITY OF TRYING TO HELP
SAVE HER PEOPLE FROM AN EVIL
MAN?

WOULD YOU RATHER BE TAKEN INTO THE KING'S HOUSE AS A YOUNG GIRL WHO WAS NEVER ALLOWED TO MARRY, OR LIVE A NORMAL LIFE OUTSIDE OF THE PALACE?

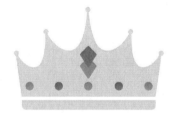

WOULD YOU RATHER REVEAL THE PLOT THAT WAS MEANT TO KILL THE KING, OR REVEAL THE PLOT THAT WAS MEANT TO KILL THE JEWS?

WOULD YOU RATHER BE PARADED THROUGH THE STREETS ON THE KING'S HORSE, OR HAVE A PRIVATE BANQUET IN THE KING'S HOUSE?

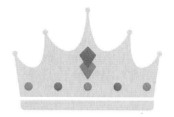

WOULD YOU RATHER BE LISTEN TO YOUR UNCLE OR CHOOSE WHAT YOU WANT TO DO?

WOULD YOU RATHER BE DRESSED IN THE KING'S ROYAL APPAREL OR BE GIVEN HIS SIGNET RING?

WOULD YOU SACRIFICE YOURSELF FOR THE SAKE OF YOUR PEOPLE OR LIVE IN LUXURY WHILE YOUR PEOPLE ARE PERSECUTED?

PLACES IN THE BIBLE

WOULD YOU RATHER HAVE BEEN
BAPTIZED IN RIVER JORDAN OR
THE RED SEA?

WOULD YOU RATHER HAVE
WISHED TO BE BORN IN
BETHLEHEM OR JERUSALEM?

WOULD YOU RATHER
VISIT ISRAEL OR
EGYPT?

WOULD YOU RATHER
CROSS THE RED SEA OR
MARCH AROUND THE RED
SEA ?

WOULD YOU RATHER SEE SOLOMON'S TEMPLE OR NOAH'S ARK?

WOULD YOU RATHER GO WITH PAUL TO VISIT ITALY OR GREECE?

WOULD YOU RATHER VISIT
THE CHURCH OF PHILIPPI
(PHILIPPIANS) OR THE CHURCH IN
CORINTH (CORINTHIANS)?

WOULD YOU RATHER BE HELD
CAPTIVE BY THE EGYPTIANS OR
ROMANS?

WOULD YOU RATHER BE AT MOUNT SINAI WHEN MOSES RECEIVED THE 10 COMMANDMENTS OR WITNESS FIRE SENT FROM HEAVEN TO CONSUME THE FALSE PROPHETS AT MOUNT CARMEL?

WOULD YOU RATHER HAVE LIVED IN THE PALACE WITH JOSEPH UNDER PHARAOH OR WITH DANIEL UNDER KING DARIUS?

THANK YOU

YOU HAVE COME TO THE END OF THIS
BOOK BUT THIS DOESN'T HAVE TO BE
THE END OF YOUR JOURNEY WITH THE
BIBLE. CHECKOUT FOREVER THANKFUL
PRESS ON AMAZON BY SCANNING THE
QR CODE BELOW.

Made in United States
North Haven, CT
15 September 2023

41412141R00057